INVESTING IN THE U.S CONSTRUCTION MARKET

A Practical Guide for Entrepreneurs, Investors, and Industry Professionals

Jeyhun Nazarov

Title: INVESTING IN THE U.S CONSTRUCTION MARKET

Author: Jeyhun Nazarov

Published by Pine Tree Press

www.pinetreepress.com

Printed in USA

Dedication

To all the builders, dreamers, and risk-takers.
Who believe that with vision, persistence, and courage,
We can build not only structures—but futures.

TABLE OF CONTENT

LEGAL, FINANCIAL & INVESTMENT DISCLAIMER

This book is provided for **educational and informational purposes only**.

It does **not** constitute legal, financial, tax, immigration, or investment advice.

Construction, real estate development, and business operations in the United States involve significant financial, legal, and regulatory risk. Laws, regulations, and market conditions vary by jurisdiction and may change without notice.

Readers are strongly advised to consult **licensed attorneys, certified public accountants, financial advisors, immigration professionals, and construction experts** before making any business or investment decisions.

The author makes no representations or guarantees regarding outcomes, profitability, immigration status, or business success.

INTRODUCTION

Why Construction Investment in the United States Matters

The United States remains one of the most attractive construction markets in the world, not because it is easy, but because it is **structured, regulated, and resilient**. Population growth, internal migration, infrastructure renewal, and persistent demand for housing and commercial space continue to create long-term opportunities across residential, commercial, and industrial construction.

For foreign investors, construction represents more than a business opportunity. It is a tangible entry point into the U.S. economy—one that combines physical assets, operational control, employment creation, and scalable growth. Unlike purely financial investments, construction forces engagement with the real systems that govern business in the United States.

At the same time, construction in the U.S. is unforgiving. Projects fail not only because of market conditions, but because of regulatory missteps, poor planning, undercapitalization, and misunderstanding of local systems. Permits, inspections, labor laws, taxation, zoning, and financing rules shape every stage of a project.

This book exists to eliminate guesswork.

It is written for:

- Foreign investors entering U.S. construction
- Entrepreneurs launching construction-related businesses
- Developers expanding into the American market
- Investors combining construction with long-term business or residency goals

This is not a motivational book.

It is a **practical guide** based on how construction investment actually works in the United States.

The goal is simple:

To help you **build legally, invest intelligently, and avoid the mistakes that cost time, money, and opportunity**.

CHAPTER 1

Understanding the U.S. Construction Market

The United States construction market is one of the most complex and opportunity-rich environments in the world. Unlike countries where construction is centralized or heavily state-controlled, the U.S. market operates through a fragmented system of **local jurisdictions, private developers, lenders, regulators, and contractors**. This decentralization creates both opportunity and risk.

For foreign investors, misunderstanding this structure is one of the most common reasons projects fail.

A Market of Local Markets

There is no single "U.S. construction market." Instead, there are thousands of local markets, each governed by its own economic conditions, zoning laws, labor availability, permitting timelines, and political realities.

Two projects that appear identical on paper can produce completely different outcomes simply because they are located in different cities or counties. Factors such as local government efficiency, community opposition, inspection practices, and infrastructure capacity can dramatically affect timelines and costs.

Successful construction investors do not analyze the United States as a whole. They study **specific cities, counties, and neighborhoods**.

Demand Drivers in U.S. Construction

Several long-term forces consistently drive construction demand in the United States.

Population growth continues to increase the need for housing, schools, healthcare facilities, and infrastructure. Internal migration reshapes markets as people move toward job centers, lower-tax states, and regions with better quality of life. Aging infrastructure requires ongoing replacement of roads, bridges, utilities, and public buildings. At the same time, logistics, e-commerce, and industrial expansion fuel demand for warehouses and manufacturing facilities.

These drivers create opportunity, but they do not eliminate risk. Construction cycles still exist, and demand can slow rapidly when interest rates rise, credit tightens, or local economies weaken.

Residential Construction: Entry Point and Trap

Residential construction is often the first entry point for foreign investors. Single-family homes, townhouses, and small multi-family buildings appear simple and familiar. Capital requirements are lower, and exit strategies are clearer.

However, residential construction can be deceptive. Margins are often thin, competition is intense, and projects are highly sensitive to interest rates and buyer sentiment. Cost overruns or permitting delays can quickly eliminate profit.

Residential construction rewards discipline, accurate budgeting, and strong local relationships. It punishes optimism and poor planning.

Commercial and Industrial Construction

Commercial and industrial construction offers greater scale and long-term potential but requires higher sophistication. These projects involve larger capital commitments, longer development timelines, and more complex financing structures.

Commercial projects are heavily scrutinized by lenders, municipalities, and community stakeholders. They require detailed feasibility studies, professional project management, and strict compliance with zoning and environmental regulations.

For investors prepared to operate at this level, commercial construction can provide stability, recurring revenue, and long-term asset value.

Labor and Cost Realities

Labor availability is one of the most critical constraints in U.S. construction. Skilled trades are in short supply in many regions, driving wages higher and increasing competition for qualified workers.

Material costs are also volatile. Supply chain disruptions, tariffs, and global demand can rapidly increase costs for lumber, steel, concrete, and mechanical systems. Successful investors assume volatility and build contingencies into budgets from the beginning.

Regulatory Environment

Regulation is not an obstacle to be avoided; it is the framework within which construction operates. Permits, inspections, codes, and compliance requirements protect safety and property values, but they also add cost and time.

Investors who view regulation as an inconvenience often face delays, fines, and project shutdowns. Those who integrate regulatory compliance into planning gain predictability and credibility.

Understanding Risk Before Opportunity

The U.S. construction market rewards investors who respect its complexity. Opportunity exists at every level, but only for those who understand how local markets function, how regulations are enforced, and how costs behave under pressure.

Construction is not about building fast.

It is about building **correctly**.

CHAPTER 2:

Entry Strategies for Foreign Investors

Entering the U.S. construction market is not a single decision but a strategic choice that defines risk exposure, control, scalability, and long-term outcomes. Foreign investors often fail not because construction is unprofitable, but because they choose an entry strategy that does not match their capital, experience, or objectives.

The United States offers multiple entry paths. Each comes with distinct legal, financial, and operational consequences.

Understanding the Role You Want to Play

Before selecting an entry strategy, investors must answer one fundamental question:

Do I want to control the business, or do I want to participate in the opportunity?

Active control provides authority and long-term growth potential, but it also requires hands-on management, compliance responsibility, and operational risk. Passive participation limits exposure but reduces influence and upside.

There is no universally correct choice.

There is only alignment—or misalignment—between strategy and reality.

Strategy One: Direct Ownership and Operation

Direct ownership involves forming or acquiring a U.S. construction company and managing operations either personally or through hired professionals. This strategy provides the highest level of control and the greatest long-term scalability.

Investors who choose direct ownership must deal with licensing, insurance, labor compliance, taxation, and regulatory oversight. They must build internal systems for estimating, project management, accounting, and risk control.

The advantage of direct ownership is structural strength. A well-run construction company can expand across projects, regions, and service lines. It can build brand value, recurring revenue, and institutional credibility.

The disadvantage is exposure. Mistakes are not shared—they are owned.

Direct ownership is best suited for investors who intend to be **actively involved** and are willing to invest time, capital, and attention into building an operation, not just completing a project.

Strategy Two: Partnerships and Joint Ventures

Many foreign investors enter the market through partnerships with local contractors, developers, or project managers. These arrangements can accelerate market entry and reduce the learning curve.

Partnerships provide access to local knowledge, existing licenses, established labor networks, and municipal relationships. They are especially useful in unfamiliar regulatory environments.

However, partnerships introduce dependency. Poorly defined authority, vague profit-sharing terms, and unclear exit provisions can lead to conflict. In construction, disputes delay projects, increase costs, and destroy value.

Successful partnerships are built on **clear legal agreements**, defined roles, transparent accounting, and aligned incentives. Investors should never rely on trust alone. Contracts exist to protect relationships, not undermine them.

Strategy Three: Project-Based Investment

Project-based investment allows foreign investors to participate financially in specific construction projects without managing daily operations. This approach limits exposure to a defined scope, timeline, and budget.

Project-based investors typically contribute capital in exchange for profit participation or fixed returns. Control is limited, but risk is more predictable.

This strategy is often used by investors who want to test the U.S. market, diversify portfolios, or maintain a passive role. It can also serve as a learning platform before committing to direct ownership.

The trade-off is influence. When problems arise, project-based investors depend on operators to resolve them.

Strategy Four: Acquisition of Existing Businesses

Some investors acquire established construction companies rather than starting from scratch. This approach offers immediate access to licenses, employees, contracts, and revenue.

Acquisitions reduce startup risk but introduce integration challenges. Hidden liabilities, poor compliance history, and cultural mismatches can undermine value if due diligence is insufficient.

A successful acquisition requires deep review of financials, contracts, insurance, and regulatory compliance.

Choosing the Right Strategy

The correct entry strategy depends on several factors:

- Available capital
- Desired level of involvement
- Risk tolerance
- Experience in construction or regulated industries
- Long-term objectives

Investors who match strategy to capability increase their chances of success. Those who pursue ambition without structure often exit the market quickly.

In U.S. construction, **how you enter** often determines **how long you survive**.

CHAPTER 3

Legal Structures And Business Formation

Legal structure is not a formality in U.S. construction—it is a **risk management tool**. The way a construction business is formed affects liability exposure, taxation, financing ability, licensing, and long-term growth. Many foreign investors underestimate this step and treat it as administrative. In construction, that mistake can be expensive.

Why Structure Matters More in Construction

Construction involves physical risk, contractual exposure, employee liability, and regulatory oversight. Accidents, disputes, and cost overruns are not theoretical—they are part of the industry. Legal structure determines **who is responsible** when something goes wrong.

A poorly structured business can expose personal assets, restrict financing options, and complicate compliance. A well-structured entity creates a buffer between risk and ownership.

Common Legal Structures Used in Construction

Limited Liability Company (LLC)

The LLC is the most common structure used by construction investors, especially at the early and mid stages. It offers limited liability protection, operational flexibility, and simplified governance.

LLCs can be structured as single-member or multi-member entities and can be taxed in different ways depending on elections made with tax authorities. This flexibility makes them attractive for both project-based and operating construction businesses.

However, flexibility does not eliminate responsibility. LLC owners must maintain proper records, separate finances, and comply with licensing and insurance requirements to preserve liability protection.

Corporations (C-Corp and S-Corp)

Corporations provide a more rigid structure and are often used for larger construction companies or businesses planning to raise outside capital. Corporations offer clearer governance rules, which lenders and institutional partners may prefer.

C-Corporations are taxed at the entity level, while S-Corporations allow pass-through taxation under specific conditions. Foreign investors should note that S-Corporations have ownership restrictions that often make them unavailable.

Corporations require more formal administration, including board meetings, reporting obligations, and compliance procedures.

Choosing the State of Formation

A common misconception is that a company can be formed anywhere without consequence. In construction, **location matters**.

Construction licenses, permits, and regulatory authority are tied to the state and locality where work is performed. Forming a company in a state solely for perceived convenience can increase costs and compliance obligations.

In many cases, the most practical choice is to form the entity in the state where construction activities will occur. This simplifies licensing, tax filings, and regulatory interaction.

Licensing and Registration Requirements

Construction is a licensed activity in many jurisdictions. Requirements may include:

- General contractor or specialty licenses
- Business registrations
- Surety bonds
- Proof of insurance
- Background checks

Licensing rules vary significantly by state and municipality. Some states license contractors at the state level, while others delegate authority to local governments.

Operating without proper licensing can result in fines, stop-work orders, contract invalidation, and personal liability. Investors should verify requirements **before** signing contracts or beginning work.

Insurance and Risk Protection

Legal structure alone does not protect against construction risk. Insurance is an essential companion.

Typical insurance coverage includes:

- General liability
- Workers' compensation
- Commercial auto
- Professional liability (where applicable)

Insurance requirements are often dictated by contracts and local regulations. Failure to maintain coverage can halt projects and expose investors to significant loss.

Structuring for Growth and Flexibility

A construction business should be structured not only for its first project, but for its second and third.

Scalability requires clarity in ownership, authority, and financial controls.

Strong legal foundations allow investors to focus on execution rather than damage control.

In U.S. construction, **structure is strategy**.

CHAPTER 4:

Immigration Considerations and Investor Status

For many foreign investors, construction investment in the United States is closely connected to long-term presence, operational control, or business expansion. While construction itself is a commercial activity, it often intersects with immigration considerations in ways that require careful planning.

One of the most common mistakes investors make is assuming that investment alone provides immigration benefits. In reality, immigration outcomes depend on **how** a business is structured and **how** the investor is involved.

Investment Does Not Automatically Mean Immigration

The United States does not grant immigration benefits simply because money is invested. Passive investment—such as contributing capital to a construction project without operational involvement—does not create eligibility for business-based status.

Immigration considerations arise when an investor is **actively directing, managing, or operating** a business. Construction businesses often meet this requirement because they demand hands-on oversight, decision-making, and responsibility for employees and contracts.

However, activity alone is not enough. The business must be legitimate, operational, and compliant.

Active Management and Business Reality

Authorities evaluate whether the investor's role reflects real business needs. This includes examining:

- Day-to-day management involvement
- Decision-making authority
- Financial control
- Responsibility for employees and operations

Artificial arrangements designed solely to support immigration goals are likely to fail. Construction businesses are particularly transparent because permits, payroll, inspections, and contracts leave extensive records.

The safest approach is to build a real business first, then align immigration strategy with that reality.

Job Creation and Economic Activity

Construction businesses naturally create employment. Workers, subcontractors, project managers, and administrative staff all contribute to economic activity. From an immigration perspective, job creation strengthens the credibility of a business.

However, employment must be legitimate. Payroll records, tax filings, and compliance with labor laws are closely scrutinized. Informal arrangements or under-the-table practices undermine both business and immigration objectives.

Compliance Beyond Immigration

Maintaining lawful presence does not replace business compliance. A construction company that violates labor laws, tax rules, or safety regulations jeopardizes its credibility regardless of immigration status.

Successful investors treat immigration planning as one component of a broader compliance strategy, not as a shortcut or substitute.

Long-Term Perspective

Construction investment is rarely a short-term endeavor. Projects take time, businesses grow gradually, and reputations are built over years.

Immigration considerations should follow the same long-term perspective.

Investors who prioritize legitimacy, transparency, and operational discipline position themselves for both business success and long-term presence in the United States.

In construction, **credibility is cumulative**.

It is earned project by project, record by record.

CHAPTER 5:

Financing Construction Projects

Financing is the backbone of every construction project in the United States. Even well-designed and well-located projects can fail if financing is poorly structured or cash flow is mismanaged. For foreign investors, understanding how construction financing works is essential, because assumptions based on other markets often do not apply in the U.S.

Construction financing is not simply about obtaining capital. It is about **timing, control, and discipline**.

Why Construction Financing Is Different

Unlike many businesses, construction requires significant upfront spending before revenue is generated. Land acquisition, design, permitting, materials, and labor costs must often be paid long before a project is completed or sold.

This creates a gap between expenses and income. Financing exists to bridge that gap, but it comes with conditions that affect every stage of the project.

In the United States, lenders, investors, and partners expect detailed planning, transparency, and strict adherence to budgets and timelines.

Common Sources of Construction Financing

Most construction projects are financed through a combination of sources rather than a single loan or investor.

Equity Capital

Equity is the investor's own capital or funds contributed by partners. Equity absorbs the highest risk but also captures the greatest potential upside. In construction, equity is often used to acquire land, cover pre-development costs, and satisfy lender requirements.

Bank Construction Loans

Banks provide construction loans that are typically short-term and tied to project milestones. These loans are released in stages, known as "draws," based on progress and inspections.

Banks focus heavily on experience, creditworthiness, and feasibility. Foreign investors may face additional scrutiny and should be prepared to provide extensive documentation.

Private and Alternative Lenders

Private lenders offer more flexibility but at higher cost. Interest rates and fees are typically higher, but approval timelines are faster. These lenders are often used when banks decline or when speed is critical.

Joint Venture Capital

Some projects are financed through joint ventures where capital is contributed by partners in exchange for profit participation. Joint ventures reduce financial burden but require clear agreements regarding control, risk, and returns.

Equity vs. Debt: Finding the Right Balance

Equity provides flexibility and reduces repayment pressure, but excessive equity can dilute ownership and reduce returns. Debt increases leverage and potential profit but introduces repayment risk and strict compliance requirements.

Successful investors balance equity and debt based on project risk, market conditions, and personal risk tolerance.

Over-leveraging is one of the most common causes of construction failure. Conservative leverage protects against market shifts and cost overruns.

Cash Flow Management and Draw Schedules

Construction financing is governed by cash flow timing. Loan proceeds are not delivered upfront. Instead, funds are released incrementally as work is completed and verified.

Delays in inspections, documentation errors, or disputes can interrupt draw schedules, creating liquidity crises. Investors must maintain reserve funds to cover gaps and unexpected costs.

Cash flow discipline is not optional—it is survival.

Lender Expectations and Documentation

Lenders expect detailed documentation, including:

- Project budgets and schedules
- Cost breakdowns
- Contracts and permits
- Insurance certificates
- Exit strategies

Foreign investors should anticipate deeper scrutiny and longer review processes. Clear communication and professional presentation improve credibility.

Risk Management Through Financing Structure

Financing decisions directly affect risk exposure. Fixed-rate loans, contingency reserves, and conservative assumptions reduce vulnerability to interest rate changes, material price increases, and delays.

Smart financing does not eliminate risk, but it controls it.

In construction, **capital alone does not build projects**.

Discipline does.

CHAPTER 6:

Land Acquisition and Zoning

Land acquisition is the foundation of every construction project. No amount of financing, design expertise, or construction skill can overcome a poorly chosen site. In the United States, land is not simply a physical asset—it is a **regulated entitlement** governed by zoning laws, environmental rules, and local political realities.

Foreign investors often underestimate this phase and treat land purchase as a real estate transaction rather than a regulatory process. This mistake can destroy projects before they begin.

Land Is Only Valuable If It Can Be Built On

A common misconception is that owning land automatically grants the right to build. In the U.S., this is rarely true. Zoning laws dictate what can be built, how large it can be, how it can be used, and under what conditions construction may proceed.

Land that appears inexpensive may be restricted by zoning, environmental protections, or infrastructure limitations. Conversely, more expensive land may offer certainty, speed, and regulatory alignment.

Successful investors evaluate land based on **buildability**, not price alone.

Understanding Zoning Classifications

Zoning classifications vary by municipality and are enforced at the local level. Common zoning categories include:

- Residential (single-family, multi-family)
- Commercial
- Industrial
- Mixed-use
- Agricultural or protected land

Each category includes detailed rules regarding density, height, setbacks, parking, and usage. Some zones permit development by right, while others require special approvals or variances.

Investors should never rely on assumptions. Zoning confirmations must be obtained in writing from local authorities.

Due Diligence Before Acquisition

Before purchasing land, investors must conduct thorough due diligence. This includes reviewing:

- Zoning ordinances and permitted uses

- Comprehensive plans and future land-use maps
- Environmental constraints (wetlands, flood zones, contamination)
- Access to utilities and infrastructure
- Easements, covenants, and restrictions

Skipping due diligence to move quickly often results in delays, redesigns, or legal disputes that cost far more than the initial savings.

Environmental and Site Conditions

Environmental issues can significantly affect cost and timeline. Soil conditions, groundwater levels, and contamination risks influence foundation design and construction methods.

Environmental assessments are not optional for serious investors. They protect against unforeseen liabilities and support financing approval.

Political and Community Considerations

Local governments and communities play a critical role in land development. Public hearings, community opposition, and political priorities can affect approvals even when zoning technically permits construction.

Engaging local professionals and understanding community dynamics can prevent conflict and accelerate approvals.

Strategic Site Selection

Strategic land acquisition balances regulatory certainty, market demand, infrastructure access, and long-term value. Experienced investors often prioritize sites that align with existing zoning and municipal objectives rather than pursuing aggressive rezoning.

In construction, the fastest projects are often the most profitable.

Land selection is not about finding the cheapest site.

It is about choosing the site that allows the project to succeed.

CHAPTER 7:

Permits, Codes, and Regulatory Compliance

Permits and regulatory compliance are often the most underestimated elements of construction investment in the United States. Many investors focus on land, financing, and design, assuming permits are procedural. In reality, permitting determines **whether**, **when**, and **how** construction can proceed.

In the U.S., construction does not begin when capital is available—it begins when permission is granted.

The Permit System Is Local, Not Federal

Construction permits are issued by **local authorities**, such as city or county building departments. Each jurisdiction operates independently, with its own procedures, timelines, fees, and enforcement standards.

A permit process that takes weeks in one city may take months in another. Understanding local practices is essential for accurate scheduling and budgeting.

Types of Permits Required

Most construction projects require multiple permits, which may include:

- Site development and grading permits
- Building permits for structural work
- Electrical, plumbing, and mechanical permits
- Fire safety and life-safety approvals
- Occupancy certificates

Each permit typically requires plan submission, review, revisions, and inspection.

Building Codes and Technical Standards

U.S. construction is governed by strict building codes designed to protect safety, durability, and public welfare. These codes regulate structural design, fire resistance, accessibility, energy efficiency, and environmental impact.

Codes are updated regularly and may be adopted differently by states and municipalities. Compliance requires coordination between architects, engineers, contractors, and inspectors.

Inspections and Enforcement

Inspections occur throughout the construction process. Inspectors verify that work matches approved plans and code requirements. Failed inspections require corrections and re-inspection, causing delays and additional costs.

Successful projects anticipate inspections and schedule work accordingly. Treating inspections as adversarial rather than procedural often leads to conflict.

Consequences of Non-Compliance

Non-compliance carries serious consequences, including:

- Stop-work orders
- Fines and penalties
- Permit revocation
- Legal liability
- Loss of financing

In severe cases, unauthorized work must be demolished.

Compliance as a Strategic Advantage

Investors who integrate compliance into planning gain predictability and credibility. Municipal authorities, lenders, and partners prefer working with developers who respect the system.

Compliance is not an obstacle—it is a competitive advantage.

In U.S. construction, **nothing moves without approval**.

Understanding the rules is not optional; it is fundamental.

CHAPTER 8:

Labor, Contractors, and Project Management

Construction is ultimately a people-driven business. Materials, equipment, and financing matter, but projects succeed or fail based on how effectively labor and contractors are managed. In the United States, labor is heavily regulated, expensive, and increasingly scarce. For foreign investors, misunderstanding labor systems is one of the fastest ways to lose control of a project.

Understanding the U.S. Construction Labor Market

The U.S. construction industry faces ongoing labor shortages, particularly in skilled trades such as carpentry, electrical work, plumbing, and mechanical systems. Demand often exceeds supply, especially during economic expansions.

Labor costs vary significantly by region. Urban areas and high-growth markets typically command higher wages, while rural regions may offer lower costs but limited availability. Investors must study local labor conditions before finalizing budgets.

Contractors vs. Employees

Construction companies typically operate using one of two labor models: hiring subcontractors or employing workers directly.

Subcontractors

Subcontractors are independent businesses responsible for specific scopes of work. They carry their own licenses, insurance, and employees. Using subcontractors reduces administrative burden but requires careful vetting and contract management.

Employees

Direct employment provides greater control but increases legal responsibility. Employers must comply with wage laws, overtime rules, payroll taxes, and workers' compensation requirements.

Misclassification—treating employees as independent contractors—is a common and costly mistake. Penalties, back wages, and legal disputes can quickly erase profits.

Licensing, Insurance, and Verification

Before engaging contractors, investors must verify licenses, insurance coverage, and compliance history. Contracts should clearly define scope, payment terms, timelines, and responsibility for permits and inspections.

Insurance requirements typically include:

- General liability
- Workers' compensation
- Commercial auto

Failure to verify coverage exposes investors to direct liability.

Project Management Discipline

Project management is the control center of construction. Effective project management includes scheduling, coordination, budgeting, quality control, and communication.

Projects without clear management structures often suffer from delays, cost overruns, and disputes. Professional project managers or construction management systems provide visibility and accountability.

Safety and Regulatory Compliance

Workplace safety is strictly regulated in U.S. construction. Employers and contractors must comply with safety standards designed to prevent injuries and fatalities.

Accidents result in more than human cost—they trigger inspections, fines, insurance claims, and reputational damage. Safety programs are not optional; they are essential risk controls.

Managing Conflict and Disputes

Disputes are common in construction. Payment disagreements, scope changes, and delays can strain relationships. Clear contracts, documentation, and communication reduce conflict and support resolution when disputes arise.

Strong management does not eliminate problems.

It limits their impact.

In construction, **people are the project**.

Managing them well is the investor's responsibility.

CHAPTER 9:

Cost Control, Risk, and Budget Discipline

In construction, profitability is rarely lost in dramatic moments. It erodes quietly—through small overruns, overlooked delays, underestimated risks, and weak controls. Cost control is not an accounting function; it is a **management discipline** that determines whether a project survives.

Foreign investors often assume that strong demand or rising property values will compensate for inefficiencies. In the U.S. construction market, this assumption is dangerous.

Understanding Where Costs Actually Come From

Construction costs extend far beyond materials and labor. A complete cost structure includes:

- Land acquisition and holding costs
- Design, engineering, and consulting fees
- Permits, impact fees, and inspections
- Labor and subcontractor payments
- Materials and equipment
- Insurance and bonding

- Financing costs and interest
- Delays, change orders, and contingencies

Projects that fail to account for indirect and soft costs often appear profitable on paper but collapse in execution.

The Role of Contingency Planning

No construction project proceeds exactly as planned. Weather, labor shortages, material price fluctuations, inspection delays, and design revisions are normal.

Contingency reserves exist to absorb uncertainty. Experienced investors allocate contingency funds from the beginning rather than hoping they will not be needed. Projects without contingency rely on luck—a poor strategy in a regulated industry.

Cost Overruns and Their Root Causes

Cost overruns typically result from:

- Incomplete or rushed design
- Unrealistic schedules
- Poor contractor coordination
- Inadequate supervision
- Regulatory surprises
- Weak change-order control

Most overruns are not caused by external forces but by internal decisions made early in the project.

Budget Discipline and Monitoring

Budget discipline requires continuous monitoring, not periodic review. Successful projects track costs in real time, compare actual spending to projections, and address deviations immediately.

Allowing overruns to accumulate in hopes of future correction often leads to financial stress and loss of control.

Risk Identification and Mitigation

Risk in construction cannot be eliminated, but it can be managed. Effective risk mitigation includes:

- Conservative assumptions
- Fixed-price or guaranteed contracts where appropriate
- Insurance coverage aligned with exposure
- Clear contractual allocation of responsibility

Risk management is proactive. Waiting for problems to surface is not management—it is reaction.

Decision-Making Under Pressure

Construction projects inevitably encounter pressure: time constraints, financial stress, and stakeholder demands. Poor decisions made under pressure often cause more damage than the original problem.

Investors who establish decision frameworks in advance—defining authority, approval thresholds, and escalation paths—maintain control when conditions deteriorate.

In construction, **discipline protects capital**.

Optimism does not.

CHAPTER 10:

Taxation in Construction Investment

Taxation is one of the least visible yet most impactful factors in construction investment. Unlike many jurisdictions with centralized tax regimes, the United States applies **layered taxation** at the federal, state, and local levels. Each layer operates independently, creating complexity that must be managed proactively.

Ignoring tax structure does not reduce tax exposure—it increases risk.

Layers of Taxation in Construction

Construction businesses may encounter multiple forms of taxation, including:

- Federal income tax
- State income or franchise tax
- Local or municipal business taxes
- Payroll taxes
- Sales and use taxes on materials and equipment

The exact mix depends on where the business operates, how it is structured, and how transactions are executed.

Business Structure and Tax Consequences

Legal structure directly influences tax outcomes. Pass-through entities may simplify reporting but can expose owners to personal tax obligations. Corporations offer clearer separation but introduce entity-level taxation.

Foreign investors must also consider withholding requirements, reporting obligations, and treaty implications. Failure to plan properly can result in unexpected liabilities and penalties.

Sales and Use Tax Exposure

Construction often triggers sales and use tax obligations on materials, equipment, and subcontracted services. Rules vary by state and are frequently misunderstood.

Improper handling of sales and use taxes can result in audits, penalties, and retroactive assessments. Accurate classification and documentation are essential.

Documentation and Compliance

Tax compliance depends on accurate records. Construction businesses must maintain detailed documentation for:

- Payroll and employment taxes

- Material purchases and invoices
- Subcontractor payments
- Depreciation of equipment and assets

Professional tax guidance is not optional in construction—it is an operational necessity.

CHAPTER 11:

Renovation - Turning Existing Buildings Into Profitable Assets

Renovation investing is one of the most reliable and accessible strategies in the U.S. construction market. Unlike ground-up development, renovation allows investors to enter projects with lower capital requirements, shorter timelines, and clearer exit strategies. In many U.S. cities, renovation has become more profitable than new construction due to zoning restrictions, labor shortages, and high land costs.

For investors—especially first-time or foreign investors—renovation offers a controlled environment where risk can be managed, costs can be forecasted more accurately, and returns can be realized faster.

1. Why Renovation Works in the U.S. Market

The U.S. has an aging housing stock. A large percentage of residential and light commercial buildings were constructed between the 1950s and 1990s. While structurally sound, many of these properties suffer from outdated layouts, inefficient materials, and cosmetic deterioration.

Renovation investing capitalizes on this gap. By upgrading interiors, exteriors, and systems, investors can significantly increase property value without changing the building footprint. This strategy benefits from constant demand driven by homeowners, renters, and small business tenants seeking modernized spaces.

2. Types of Renovation Investments

Not all renovations are equal. Successful investors understand which type aligns with their budget, experience, and exit plan.

Cosmetic Renovations

These include painting, flooring, lighting, kitchen cabinet refacing, and bathroom upgrades. Cosmetic renovations offer fast turnaround and high visual impact, making them ideal for resale or short-term rentals.

Functional Renovations

Functional upgrades involve plumbing, electrical systems, HVAC, roofing, and insulation. These projects require more expertise but significantly improve long-term value and reduce future maintenance costs.

Structural & Layout Renovations

Wall removals, room reconfigurations, and additions fall into this category. While more capital-intensive, these renovations can transform underperforming properties into premium assets.

3. Renovation Budgeting: Where Investors Make or Lose Money

Budget discipline determines profitability. Many renovation projects fail not because of poor design, but because of cost overruns.

A professional renovation budget includes:

- Acquisition cost
- Demolition and labor
- Materials and finishes
- Permits and inspections
- Contingency (typically 10–15%)

Experienced investors avoid over-improving properties. Renovation scope should match neighborhood standards. Spending luxury-level budgets in mid-range neighborhoods rarely produces proportional returns.

4. Materials Selection: Investment, Not Decoration

Renovation investors think differently about materials. The goal is durability, market appeal, and cost efficiency—not personal taste.

Common high-ROI material choices include:

- Engineered flooring over solid hardwood
- Fiber cement or composite siding instead of traditional wood
- Quartz countertops instead of natural stone
- Pre-finished wall panels for faster installation

Smart material selection reduces installation time, warranty issues, and long-term maintenance, directly impacting net profit.

5. Permits, Codes, and Inspections

One of the most common mistakes in renovation investing is underestimating regulatory requirements. Each city and county in the U.S. has its own permitting rules, and violations can stop a project entirely.

Investors must understand when permits are required—especially for electrical, plumbing, structural changes, and exterior modifications. Skipping permits may save money short-term but can cause serious legal and resale issues later.

6. Working With Contractors

Renovation success depends heavily on contractor performance. Investors should work only with licensed and insured professionals, using written contracts that define scope, timeline, and payment milestones.

Best practices include:

- Avoiding large upfront payments
- Linking payments to completed stages
- Using lien waivers
- Conducting frequent site inspections

Clear communication and documentation prevent disputes and delays.

7. Timeline Management and Delays

Time is money in renovation investing. Every additional week increases holding costs such as mortgage payments, insurance, and utilities.

Common causes of delays include:

- Material backorders
- Poor scheduling
- Labor shortages
- Change orders

Successful investors plan realistic timelines and maintain buffer periods to protect profitability.

8. Exit Strategies for Renovation Projects

Renovation investors typically choose between three exit paths:

- Resale (Fix & Flip) – Fast capital recovery and profit realization
- Rent & Hold – Long-term cash flow with appreciation

- Refinance & Reinvest – Leveraging increased value to fund new projects

The exit strategy should be defined before renovation begins, as it directly influences design, materials, and budget decisions.

9. Renovation Risks and How to Manage Them

Renovation investing carries risks, including hidden structural issues, cost overruns, and market shifts. Risk is managed through:

- Thorough inspections before purchase
- Conservative budgeting
- Fixed-price contracts where possible
- Insurance coverage
- Local market knowledge

Investors who plan for problems rarely suffer major losses.

10. Renovation as a Long-Term Strategy

For many investors, renovation is not a one-time project but a repeatable business model. By standardizing designs, material selections, and contractor teams, investors can scale renovation operations across multiple properties.

Renovation investing rewards discipline, patience, and strategic thinking. In the U.S. market, it remains one of the most practical and resilient paths to building wealth in construction.

CHAPTER 12:

Investing in the Building Materials Market in the United States

Investing in the building materials market is one of the most stable and scalable strategies within the U.S. construction ecosystem. Unlike property development, which is project-based and capital-intensive, building materials investing is demand-driven, repeatable, and less exposed to zoning, entitlement, and construction delays.

The U.S. construction industry relies on a constant flow of materials to support residential housing, renovation, infrastructure, and commercial development. As long as buildings are constructed, repaired, or upgraded, the demand for building materials remains consistent—even during economic slowdowns.

1. Why Building Materials Investing Is Attractive

Building materials investing offers several advantages compared to traditional real estate or construction projects:

- Lower entry barriers compared to land development
- Faster inventory turnover and cash flow
- Diversified customer base (contractors, developers, homeowners)
- Reduced exposure to permitting and entitlement risk
- Scalability without owning property

For many investors, building materials represent a **business-backed investment**, where value is created through sourcing, pricing, logistics, and relationships rather than speculation.

2. Understanding Market Demand

Demand in the building materials market is driven by three main segments:

New Construction

Residential and commercial developments require large volumes of structural and finishing materials. While sensitive to interest rates, this segment creates bulk, long-term demand.

Renovation and Remodeling

Renovation is the most resilient segment. Aging housing stock, lifestyle upgrades, and energy-efficiency improvements create continuous demand regardless of economic cycles.

Infrastructure and Public Projects

Government-funded projects support baseline demand for materials such as cement-based products, insulation, and exterior systems.

Successful investors track which segment is strongest in their region and align inventory accordingly.

3. Key Building Material Categories for Investors

Not all materials offer equal investment potential. High-performing categories typically share durability, repeat demand, and predictable installation cycles.

Common investment-focused categories include:

- Exterior cladding and siding systems
- Composite decking and fencing
- Fiber cement and engineered panels
- Interior wall panels and acoustic solutions
- Insulation and weather-resistant materials

These products balance durability, compliance with U.S. building codes, and market acceptance.

4. Importing vs. Domestic Sourcing

Investors must decide between importing materials or sourcing domestically.

Imported Materials often offer:

- Lower manufacturing costs
- Broader design options
- Private-label opportunities

However, they also involve:

- Tariffs and duties
- Freight and port delays
- Currency risk

Domestic Materials provide:

- Faster delivery
- Easier compliance
- Stronger brand recognition

Many successful investors use a hybrid model—importing select products while sourcing others locally to balance risk and cash flow.

5. Pricing Strategy and Profit Margins

Profitability in building materials investing depends more on pricing discipline than on volume alone.

Investors must understand:

- Wholesale vs retail margin structures
- Contractor pricing expectations
- Volume discount thresholds
- Competitive market pricing

Overpricing leads to stagnant inventory, while under-pricing erodes margins. Sustainable businesses focus on **consistent margins**, not aggressive short-term gains.

6. Inventory, Warehousing, and Logistics

Inventory management is one of the most critical operational aspects of materials investing.

Key considerations include:

- Inventory turnover rates
- Storage costs and damage risk
- Local warehousing vs third-party logistics (3PL)
- Container-sized purchasing vs partial shipments

Poor inventory control ties up capital and reduces flexibility. High-performing investors prioritize fast-moving SKUs and standardized product lines.

7. Sales Channels and Customer Base

Building materials investors rarely rely on a single sales channel.

Common channels include:

- Contractors and subcontractors
- Developers and builders
- Architects and designers
- Retail showrooms
- B2B online sales

Diversifying sales channels reduces dependency on any single customer group and stabilizes revenue.

8. Legal, Insurance, and Compliance Considerations

Materials investors must operate within U.S. legal and regulatory frameworks, including:

- Business registration and tax compliance
- Product liability insurance
- Warranty and specification accuracy
- Contract terms and payment protection

Ignoring legal fundamentals exposes investors to lawsuits and financial losses that can outweigh profits.

9. Risks in Building Materials Investing

While more stable than construction projects, building materials investing carries its own risks:

- Price volatility due to supply chain disruptions
- Non-paying customers
- Overstocking slow-moving products
- Regulatory or tariff changes

Risk management strategies include diversified sourcing, credit control policies, insurance coverage, and conservative purchasing.

10. Scaling a Building Materials Investment

Scalability is one of the strongest advantages of this sector. Investors can grow by:

- Expanding product categories
- Entering new geographic markets
- Building private-label brands
- Securing exclusive distribution agreements

Unlike property-based investing, scaling does not require proportional capital increases when systems and relationships are optimized.

Conclusion: Building Materials as a Long-Term Investment Strategy

Investing in the building materials market is not speculative—it is operational. Success depends on understanding demand, managing costs, and building long-term relationships rather than betting on market timing.

For investors seeking a durable, repeatable, and scalable position within the U.S. construction industry, building materials investing offers a balanced path between entrepreneurship and asset-based returns.

CHAPTER 13:

Scaling and Long-Term Growth

Construction investment is rarely about a single project. Long-term success requires scalability, discipline, and strategic growth. Expanding too quickly can be as dangerous as failing to expand at all.

Growth should be **intentional**, not reactive.

From Projects to Platforms

Early construction ventures often focus on individual projects. Sustainable businesses evolve into platforms capable of executing multiple projects simultaneously.

This transition requires systems: standardized processes, reliable management, and financial controls. Growth without systems amplifies risk.

Reputation as an Asset

In construction, reputation is currency. Municipal authorities, lenders, contractors, and suppliers prefer to work with operators who demonstrate reliability and compliance.

Reputation is built slowly and lost quickly. Ethical practices, transparent communication, and consistent performance create long-term advantage.

Geographic and Service Expansion

Expansion may involve entering new markets or offering additional services. Both strategies require careful analysis of regulatory differences, labor availability, and competitive dynamics.

Growth that ignores local conditions often fails.

CHAPTER 14:

Common Mistakes and How to Avoid Them

Construction failures are rarely caused by a single catastrophic event. They result from **patterns of poor decision-making**.

Recurring Errors

Common mistakes include:

- Underestimating regulatory complexity
- Inadequate capitalization
- Poor partner selection
- Weak contracts
- Ignoring professional advice

Each mistake compounds risk and reduces margin.

Learning Through Discipline

Successful investors treat mistakes as data, not disasters. They analyze failures, adjust systems, and improve decision-making.

Construction rewards preparation and punishes assumption.

CONCLUSION

Building Long-Term Value in the United States

Construction investment in the United States offers substantial opportunity for those willing to operate within a structured, regulated environment.

This market rewards:

- Compliance over shortcuts
- Planning over speculation
- Discipline over optimism
- Long-term vision over quick profit

Foreign investors who understand local systems, respect regulatory frameworks, and build strong operational foundations can create durable businesses with lasting value.

Construction success is not accidental.

It is built—carefully, deliberately, and project by project.

ABOUT THE AUTHOR

Jeyhun Nazarov is an entrepreneur and building materials professional with extensive experience in construction supply, international sourcing, and market development. He is the founder of **Norm Supply**, a company focused on modern exterior building solutions including composite fencing, decking, architectural cladding systems, and innovative façade materials designed for contemporary construction.

Earlier in his career, Jeyhun founded and operated a **steel structure** company, where he gained hands-on experience in structural systems, project development, and the practical realities of the construction industry. This early experience provided him with a deep understanding of how buildings are designed, engineered, and brought to life in real-world construction environments.

Over the years, Jeyhun has worked across multiple areas of the building materials sector, including product development, international sourcing, supply chain management, and market expansion. His work has involved collaborating with manufacturers, contractors, and distributors while navigating global manufacturing networks and the evolving demands of the U.S. construction market.

Through his entrepreneurial journey, he has developed a practical perspective on how construction materials businesses operate—from manufacturing and logistics to marketing and distribution. With a focus on innovation and efficiency, he continues to explore new materials, systems, and opportunities that shape the future of modern construction.

Through this book, Jeyhun shares insights drawn from his experience to help investors, entrepreneurs, and industry professionals better understand the opportunities within the construction and building materials industry.

www.ingramcontent.com/pod-product-compliance
Lightning Source LLC
LaVergne TN
LVHW010841120826
845149LV00020B/3436

* 9 7 8 1 9 6 9 6 4 9 8 7 5 *